IMAGES OF ENGLAND

NEWCASTLE UPON TYNE

The glorious Pearl Assurance building on the corner of New Bridge Street and Northumberland Street, *c.* 1910.

IMAGES OF ENGLAND

NEWCASTLE UPON TYNE

PETER HEPPLEWHITE

The History Press

Decorations for the Coronation of King George VI, Northumberland Street, 1937.

First published in 1999 by Tempus Publishing

Reprinted 2002, 2005

Reprinted in 2008 by
The History Press
The Mill, Brimscombe Port,
Stroud, Gloucestershire, GL5 2QG
www.thehistorypress.co.uk

Reprinted 2011, 2013

British Library Cataloguing in Publication Data.
A catalogue record for this book is available from the British Library.

ISBN 978 0 7524 1598 7

Typesetting and origination by
Tempus Publishing Limited.
Printed in Great Britain.

Contents

Eight happy bundles from the maternity ward of Newcastle General Hospital, *c.* 1920.

Acknowledgements

I would like to thank the many individuals and organizations who have donated photographs to Tyne and Wear Archives Service. Special thanks go to Children North East, Mr G.R. Morley, Newcastle upon Tyne Hospitals NHS Trust, Northumbria Water, Siemens Power Generation Ltd and Vickers Defence Systems. Practical help from other Archives staff speeded the completion of this book, especially the many suggestions from Mark Stephens and the long hours of photography from Matthew Parsons.

Introduction

Tyne and Wear Archives Service cares for the records of five districts – Gateshead, Sunderland, North Tyneside, South Tyneside and Newcastle. The archives are housed in specially equipped and converted accommodation in Blandford House, Newcastle. Together they present one of the largest collections for local history in the country, though many items also have national and even international significance. The records cover eight miles of shelves and are still growing fast.

Documents held by the Archives have been deposited over the past twenty-five years by public and private institutions and individuals alike. The variety of hand-written, printed and pictorial material is vast, ranging from enormous collections such as the business records of Vickers Defence Systems to the few worn pages of a First World War diary hastily scribbled on the Ypres front in 1916. Photographs feature prominently in many of the collections.

Newcastle is the regional capital of the North East and has a long and distinguished history. The city has been an outpost of the Roman Empire, a Norman frontier town, a prominent Tudor trading community and a centre of mining, shipbuilding and engineering during the industrial age that sent Geordie products around the world. This legacy is still visible in the modern city, now undergoing redevelopment to meet the challenges of the twenty-first century. Since the 1850s this cycle of change and redevelopment has been comprehensively photographed.

Selecting 200 images from the thousands in Tyne and Wear Archives was daunting. One aim was to include many shots that had not been published before. A second was to show the experiences of the people, 'in sickness and in health', rather than concentrating simply on the buildings. It is in depicting the vigorous social life of the city that the photographs of the Archives Service are richest and as such it is worth giving background details of a few of the more remarkable collections.

Until the 1960s and the growing impact of the service sector of the economy, Newcastle prospered and suffered with the traditional heavy industries of the region. In the forefront was Armstrong's, now Vickers Defence Systems. This great engineering and armaments company was founded by William Armstrong on a $5\frac{1}{2}$ acre site in the open countryside of Elswick in 1847. By 1900, when William (now Lord) Armstrong died, the vast works stretched across 230 acres and employed 25,000 men. Company photographs and plans record products as varied as warships, tanks, pit-cages and marine crankshafts (see pp. 24, 25, 81 and 82). Pictures of the workforce run from the formal images of directors to shots of the lively social life of the metal-bashers (see p. 83).

Over the years the Archives Service has catalogued extensive collections from hospitals which are now closed or managed by Newcastle upon Tyne Hospitals NHS Trust. These illustrate the struggle to provide comprehensive healthcare before the Welfare State was founded in the late 1940s. Many city families had reason to be grateful to historic institutions such as the RVI with its origins in the old infirmary built in 1751 (pp. 108-109) or Newcastle General which evolved from the nineteenth-century Workhouse (pp. 110-111).

The various departments of the City Council have recorded aspects of their own work and together they offer hundreds of shots of local authority activities. The inter-war years especially were a time of struggle and pride. Major slum clearance and housing programmes marked the effort to provide homes fit for heroes (p. 50); the Edwardian tram system was replaced by innovative trolley buses (pp. 63-64 and 70); while regular education weeks drew public attention to the varied provision for different age ranges and abilities (p. 80). In contrast to the modern preoccupation with testing, the handbook for the 1925 Education Week roundly declared, 'Happiness is the keynote of the infant schools. Everything is done to make the little child happy in his environment and happy in his work.'

This selection of photographs is offered in the hope that they will entertain and inform. Archive staff would be most grateful to hear of any errors or omissions. Even better, should you be reading this introduction and wondering what to do with those old photos of grandpa's in the loft, give the Archives first refusal before they end up in the bin.

The Chancellor's Head Inn, Newgate Street, c. 1955. It was then owned by Robert Deuchar Ltd.

One

The Historic City

The Black Gate and the Castle, looking south towards the High Level Bridge, c. 1920. The late twelfth-century keep was restored by John Dobson in 1847. The distinctive battlements and turrets are Victorian rather than medieval. The elaborate shop in the centre of the image is Doric Stores, selling wines, spirits and tobacco.

The Black Gate in 1875. This fortified gateway was built between 1247 and 1250. At the end of the nineteenth century the Black Gate area was a slum, known for its second-hand clothing, boot, clog and shoe shops. The upper floors were let off in tenements. R.J. Charlton, describing Newcastle in 1885, wrote, 'The children lay about in the gutters, and enjoy their dirty freedom in the company of a few bedraggled fowls', a comment borne out in this shot. Beall's was a stone yard in front of the Black Gate.

The Black Gate, *c.* 1880. A young woman leans against the doorway of a cobbler's shop. Christie's Directory for 1876/77 lists four shoemakers, two tailors and four clothes dealers in the Gate.

The Black Gate in 1886. Shortly after this shot was taken, it was restored, the tenants were moved out and the gateway was converted into a museum for the Society of Antiquaries. The Head of the Side and St Nicholas' Cathedral stand in the background.

The Castle Garth from the top of Dog Leap Stairs, looking north-west, *c.* 1880. Charlton describes it as 'a narrow, curved street of tumbled down, rickety houses, with smoke-blackened weather boards.... There is an air of squalor and decay over the whole place.' In contrast, the elegant spire of the cathedral adds a misty elegance.

Below opposite: The Sandhill Café on the ground floor of 41 Sandhill, part of Bessie Surtee's House, *c.* 1930. It now houses offices for English Heritage. In 1931 the house was bought by the Rt Hon. S.R. Vereker, later Viscount Gort, a descendant of the famous Bessie. Partly because of the family link, he wanted to convert the building into a fine town residence. The engineer employed to supervise the restoration, R.F. Wilkinson, recalled the chequered career of the property: 'From being mansions these houses have been malsters, manufacturing chemist, lodging house, meeting place and a seamen's mission. The shops have been 1d Gaffs [a cheap music hall], wax works, seed shop, refreshment house and warehouse. When I started, the seamen's mission was still there. I am sorry to say the majority of frequenters were not seamen.'

Cobblers' shops, with distinctive
signs, towards the top of Castle
Stairs, *c*. 1890. The Stairs still lead
their steep way down to the Close,
near the end of the Swing Bridge.
In the late Victorian period they
were lined with second-hand boot
and shoe shops. The premises in
the photograph belonged to one of
Newcastle's oldest guilds, Trinity
House.

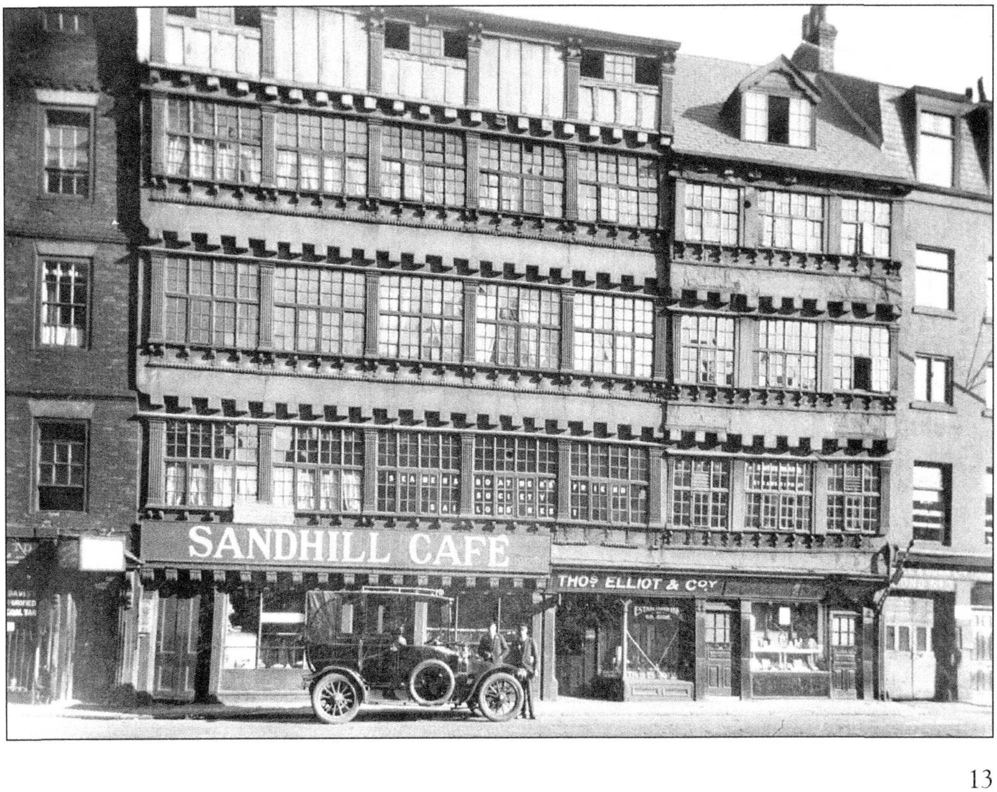

The Cooperage, no. 32 The Close, in 1886. The premises, used by John Arthur to make barrels, were once the warehouses and offices of wealthy merchants who wanted easy access to the river.

The Cooperage and a view of the Long Stairs, *c*. 1890. The blurred sign on the second floor advertises the premises of J.W. Mawson, dunnage mat merchant. Today the Cooperage is a thriving pub.

A view from the Tuthill stairs of a
surviving Elizabethan mansion, *c.* 1880.
This was used as a Baptist chapel during
the late Victorian period.

Looking up the Foot of the Side, *c.* 1880. The Side was the main medieval street from the bridge
to the higher part of the town.

Looking east, from the Head of the Side, *c.* 1880. Number 86, famously known as the birthplace of Admiral Collingwood, stands in the foreground. When this shot was taken it was a pub, the Meter's Arms.

Numbers 33-41 The Side, premises of J. Nicholson (fruiterer) and Lockharts Cocoa Rooms, *c.* 1882.

St Nicholas' Cathedral from Collingwood Street, *c.* 1885. The horse-drawn cab stand in the foreground occupies the site of the modern St Nicholas Square. The crane in Beall's masonry yard can be seen between the Black Gate and the Castle. The fifteenth-century steeple is 59m (193ft) high. William Grey, Newcastle's first historian, wrote in 1649 that it 'lifteth up a head of majesty high above the rest, as a cypresse tree above the low shrubs'. Even against today's cluttered skyline it remains a landmark for homecoming Geordies.

Sandgate looking east, *c.* 1882. The view includes the Three Bulls' Heads and John Spire's lodging house on the corner of Milk Market. One of the unique pants, or public standpipes, can be seen in the foreground. Sandgate, formerly the haunt of keelmen, was a fast-changing area of Irish migrants in the late Victorian period.

Blackfriars, 22 May 1957. Blackfriars was a Dominican monastery, founded in around 1260 and closed during the Reformation. The buildings were subsequently used by the Guilds and gradually fell into disrepair. By the 1950s they were derelict but were thankfully saved by a restoration programme in the 1970s.

Two

Riverside and Bridges

An aerial view of the City looking northwards, *c.* 1930. The Great North Road can be seen in the top left background.

Tyne General Ferry Company Steamers in around 1905, with the High Level and Swing bridges in the background. The ferries ran from the Newcastle landing, criss-crossing the river to the North Pier at Tynemouth. In its last years the company was strangled by the NER electric railway to Tynemouth, but fought back bravely. How's this for a hard sell? 'Those parents who live within reasonable reach of the Tyne, and do not take their children to Tynemouth and back by water … are withholding from them a present enjoyment and a life-long memory.'

A northbound train crosses the High Level Bridge, c. 1950. This landmark bridge was designed by Robert Stephenson. Work began in 1846 and was completed in 1849. The road is 85ft and the railway 112ft above high water. The overall length is 1,400ft.

The Swing Bridge, seen here in around 1920, stands on the site of the Roman, medieval and Georgian bridges. It was built by W.G. Armstrong & Co. between 1868 and 1876. The wrought-iron superstructure is 281ft long, weighs 1,450 tons and swings open on cast-iron rollers to allow vessels to pass. It is rarely used today, but was essential to allow sea-going vessels passage from Armstrong's Elswick shipyards (see pp. 24 and 25).

A view from the High Level Bridge down-river, c. 1910. Notice the busy quayside and the number of people walking across the Swing Bridge.

The New Tyne Road Bridge was designed by Mott, Hay and Anderson, with local architect R. Dick Burns responsible for the towers. The contract was awarded to Dorman Long and Co. Ltd, who submitted a tender of £30,000 less than their closest rival.

Since the River Tyne Commissioners insisted on full navigational clearance for river traffic, the designers came up with a single-span arch 531ft long, carrying a suspended road deck 84ft above high water. This was a reduced version of the design for the Sydney Harbour bridge but the largest in Britain when opened.

Work began in August 1925 and was completed in three years. With the arch advancing from both banks of the river, the gap in the span was closed 25 February 1928. The bridge was officially opened by HM King George V on 10 October 1928.

This brooding picture shows HMS *Superb* passing the Swing Bridge in 1907. She was a stunning example of a Tyneside warship, a Bellerophon class battleship built in Armstrong's

Elswick Yard and engined by Wallsend Slipway with 23,000hp Parsons turbines.

A schooner unloading timber in midstream *c.* 1920. Sailing ships were still a common sight on the Tyne. The Hamburg-Rotterdam ferry terminal is on the left in the background.

A rare early photograph of the Quayside before the Great Fire of 1854, taken by John Parry in 1848.

A busy Quayside scene, *c.* 1910. Although coal was not shipped from the Quayside, the area was the commercial centre of the Great Northern Coalfield. The coalfitters, the middlemen between the colliery owners and the shippers, were largely based here. The Newcastle ferry landing stage can be seen on the extreme right. The buildings on the left were demolished to make way for the New Tyne Bridge.

Sandhill looking north west from the Guildhall towards the High Level Bridge. This view from around 1900 includes nos 38-41, premises of B.J. Sutherland and Co., flour, grain and provisions merchant; H. & W. Robertson, hay and straw merchants; J. Richardson, hairdresser; J. Edminson, corn and salt dealer and Newton and Co., India rubber merchants.

A crowd round a fish seller probably near the fishmarket, *c.* 1885. Notice the barefoot boy. It was common for poor children to be barefoot in the summer, until their feet had stopped growing.

28

A view from the Tyne Bridge on to the busy Quayside market, *c. 1930*. Notice the pigs being driven along. A good deal of livestock was still imported and exported from the Quayside.

The Exchange Buildings, seen here around 1861, were a monument to Victorian enterprise. They formed part of the redevelopment of the Quayside after the great fire of 1854; early tenants were largely involved in shipping, maritime insurance and the coal trade. One of the famous Armstrong hydraulic cranes can be seen in the centre of the photograph.

By 1979 the old Redheugh Bridge was almost unusable to all but light traffic because of the ravages of age and corrosion. The new pre-stressed concrete road bridge was opened by HRH Diana, Princess of Wales, in 1983. This shot shows the demolition of the old bridge after completion of the new one.

In this view demolition is almost complete. The abutments of the old bridge stand in stark contrast to the gleaming concrete of its successor. The main span of the New Redheugh Bridge measures 160m, with two side spans of 100m. It can carry an abnormal load up to 4,000 tonnes and is expected to last until the end of the twenty-first century.

Three

City Streets

The bottom of Northumberland Street in around 1900, showing the buildings on the east side from Saville Row to Northumberland Place. There is a coach and pair waiting with an elegantly attired coachman.

Northumberland Street, *c.* 1920. It is hard to imagine that the Great North Road from London to Edinburgh ran through the middle of this busy shopping street.

Grey Street on a rainy and muddy day in 1890. Horse traffic, with ample dung, often made Victorian streets treacherous to cross. This photograph looks up towards Grey's Monument, with the portico of the Theatre Royal on the upper right.

A more expansive view from a similar date. Grey Street is widely held to be the finest thoroughfare in Newcastle, the peak of the 'Tyneside Classical' developments masterminded by the builder Richard Grainger between 1834 and 1839. His master-stroke was to buy and demolish Anderson Place, a mansion with twelve acres of ground in the city centre. This became the basis for his ambitious new town scheme.

Grainger Street West, looking up from Neville Street, c. 1920. The fifteenth-century tower of St John the Baptist's church stands opposite the Newcastle Savings Bank. Grainger's memorial inside the Church reads: 'A citizen of Newcastle ... does not need to be reminded of [his] genius.... A stranger is referred to the principal streets in the centre of this city.'

Grainger Street in around 1880 (above) and 1910 (below). Fashions have changed and the horse-drawn trams have been replaced by electric traction. On the left Isaac Walton's Tailors and Outfitters occupy nos 23-31. The fine ribbed dome of the Exchange Building is on the right. In the background stands Grey's monument, the focus of 'Grainger Town'. The column, 135ft high, was erected in 1838 to commemorate Earl Grey and his role in the passing of the 1832 Reform Act, the beginning of modern democracy in Britain.

Barras Bridge, *c.* 1925, so called because it was once a bridge over a deep dene. The stone arch is still under the road. On the left is St Thomas' church, designed by John Dobson and built between 1827 and 1830.

The west side of Percy Street from the corner of Gallowgate to no. 17, *c.* 1880. This photograph includes the premises of W. Fenwick, grocer; John Mills, furniture dealer; Mary Gibson, milliner; and Anne McGee, marine store dealer.

Percy Street looking south, with a splendid array of advertisements on the gable-end. Charlton, writing in 1885, comments: 'It has, even now, an old-fashioned appearance, like the high street of some country town, with its old cottages, interspersed amongst the quiet and dull-looking houses of more modern times.'

A snapshot of St Thomas' churchyard on a bright spring day, *c.* 1950. A group of women enjoy the sun by the memorial to the Royal Tank Regiment, which was erected in around 1920. The figure of St George stands guard overhead.

A view across Haymarket to St Thomas' church, 1907. The South African war memorial dominates the scene. A workman is putting the finishing touches to the base of the monument. Above, a winged Victory stands on a tapered, octagonal column over 70ft high.

Looking up Newgate Street from Grainger Street, on as far as Low Friar Street, in May 1910. Newgate was the medieval market street of Newcastle. This photograph mainly shows the south side, including the Empire Palace theatre.

The old Central Library, New Bridge Street, *c.* 1910. This fine building, opened in 1884, stood on the site of Carliol Tower, part of the medieval town wall. In turn, it fell victim to development and was demolished in 1968 to make way for John Dobson Street.

The Walker tram on Blackett Street, *c.* 1905. The Pearl Assurance building of 1904 can be seen on the corner with Northumberland Street. A fun turret, together with the dome representing a gigantic pearl, made this an eye-catching structure. A pity about its bland replacement!

Low Friar Street at the junction with Dispensary Lane in 1904. This is nicely dated by the poster for the Brass Band Contest on the gable end. These properties were owned by the Cordwainers' Guild.

The Bigg Market, looking towards Newgate Street, *c.* 1950. This was the medieval barley (bigg) market, sometimes called 'The Oate Market'. The red sandstone Rutherford Memorial fountain, moved from St Nicholas' Square in 1903, stands in the centre of the photograph. Dr John Hunter Rutherford was a radical doctor and preacher. He pioneered free secondary and technical education in the city. Those wanting to experience Newcastle as a 'party' city must include a weekend night out on the Bigg Market. Be brave!

The bottom of Westgate Road looking towards Collingwood Street, *c.* 1920. On the left is Neville Hall, offices and library of the North of England Institute of Mining and Mechanical Engineers. The Italianate Collingwood Buildings, mid-right, were completed in 1903 for Barclays Bank. Collingwood Street was constructed in 1810 and named after local hero Cuthbert Collingwood, Nelson's most trusted admiral.

George Stephenson's Monument, *c.* 1920. Designed by John Lough, the monument was erected in 1862. Oddly, Stephenson's bronze figure stands with his back to Central station. The four classical figures at his feet represent industrial skills. Stephenson stands on the site of the medieval Hospital of St Mary the Virgin, later converted into the Royal Grammar School and demolished in 1844 to make way for Neville Street.

A snapshot of the Side, 1928.

Four
Housing Contrasts

Jesmond Towers, the south front and entrance, 1910. This was the elegant home of the Walker shipbuilder C.W. Mitchell. Mitchell, a Scotsman, founded his yard in 1851 and began to build warships in tandem with W.G. Armstrong's Elswick works in 1867. Mitchell's built the vessels and Armstrong's manufactured and fitted the weapons.

The hall, Jesmond Towers, 1910.

The splendid billiard room at Jesmond Towers. Note the heating pipes under the table.

A step down the ladder of industrial entrepreneurs, the Richardson family built The Gables in the mid-1870s. This fine Victorian villa, on Elswick Road, was close to their leather works on the banks of the Tyne. Notice the observatory in the front garden. The Richardsons were Quakers, kindly but strict employers. The company motto was 'Let every man find his work and do it'.

The Richardson family by the main entrance to The Gables, c. 1875.

Emma and Thomas Pumphrey enjoy their garden in Summerhill Grove, 1908. The Pumphreys were another successful Quaker family, making their fortune from a wholesale grocery and tea-dealing business. Their Continental roast coffee was renowned.

Emma and Thomas in their 'cosy' chairs, 1908. This also gives us a rare interior view of a middle-class home. Note the electric light.

Water Street, Elswick, on a bright summer day, *c.* 1930. The next four pictures show company houses owned by Richardson's leather works. In 1930 the rent for a two bedroomed house was 6s per week. The houses were well maintained. Repairs were done by works' joiners, brickies and plumbers. When electricity was installed it was done by company electricians. Many residents regretted the demolition of the properties in the 1970s, insisting that improvement would have been a better planning strategy.

Residents pose in the back lane between Shumac Street and Water Street.

Dunn Street, *c.* 1930.

The narrow alley at the back of Dunn Street,
c. 1930. When Richardsons finally closed in
1970, 180 people lost their jobs and a close-knit
way of life ended for a small community.

Old houses in the Buckingham Street area and their replacements, early 1930s. During this period the council rehoused around 30,000 people in slum clearance projects. Lice were a common problem and a cyanide disinfestation station was opened in Merley Road, Walker, to delouse furniture from slum properties before it was moved into new homes.

Five

Serving the Public

The Town Hall, seen here in 1910, was built between 1858 and 1863 at a cost of £50,000. It was never a favourite building with the Victorian public who felt it lacked the grandeur that should mark the headquarters of a major city.

Central Library and the Laing Art Gallery, New Bridge Street, *c.* 1910. The library was opened in 1880 by Alderman Joseph Cowan, who withdrew the first book. Appropriately for such a radical politician he chose J.S. Mill's tract *On Liberty*. It is easy to forget that public libraries marked a revolution in Victorian education and entertainment. For many years the building was known by its older and more meaningful title, the Free Library. Sadly the library was demolished in 1968/69 to make way for John Dobson Street.

Public wash houses, Gallowgate, in around 1970, shortly before their demolition. These Victorian amenities provided an important health service well into the twentieth century. In the year ending 30 March 1925, for example, 58,000 people used the slipper baths or washing tubs.

The Mayor, John Grantham, inspects the police on Lord Mayor's Sunday, 16 November 1936. Newcastle proudly operated a city police force from 1836 to 1969.

A stylish artist's impression of the new police headquarters, courts and fire station, opened on the junction of Market Street and Pilgrim Street in 1933. This ushered in a new controversial style of policing. Six local stations were closed to avoid maintenance and renovation costs and replaced by police boxes. These innovations led to a cut of forty-nine men. One aim was to present a less formal view of the police to the public. There were no uniformed officers mounting guard on the entrance, 'only a mahogany revolving door [leading to a] spacious general office ... with all the convenience of a large banking or insurance hall.'

A view of the fire station courtyard, 1933. Staff facilities included accommodation for twenty-one married police-firemen, a children's playground on the roof, a gymnasium and small cinema. Look out for the griffins above the fire appliance doors on Pilgrim Street: they represent Power, Watchfulness and Swiftness.

Carliol House, Pilgrim Street, lit up for a night time publicity photograph in 1934. Carliol House was opened in 1927 as the head office and showrooms of the pioneering North Eastern Electric Supply Company. The 1934 Annual Report proudly boasted that 19,289 new customers had been connected to the company's mains – one household every five minutes of the working day.

Newcastle and Gateshead Water Company's narrow gauge railway at Spittlehope Crossing, on the Rede pipeline, *c.* 1900. Newcastle was a thirsty industrial city and as the nineteenth century drew to a close the Water Company embarked on its most ambitious construction project, Catcleugh Reservoir. A 27-mile temporary railway carried workers and materials alongside the pipeline from Catcleugh to Hallington reservoirs.

Lowering a 33-inch water main along Armstrong Road, *c.* 1900. This was a feeder pipe for the city.

The prize-winning football team of Todd's Nook Board School, 1896. The first Newcastle School Board was elected in January 1871 and the first Board School, in Westmorland Road, was opened in 1875. Todd's Nook School was opened in 1891.

The 6+ class at Canning Street School, 1906. The toys are probably models used for object lessons. Whilst most children are in their best clothes for the photograph, the poverty of others is clear. Note the ragged clothes of the third boy from the left in the middle row.

Boys playing ball at the Royal Victoria School for the Blind, 1925. The boys at the sides are listening to discover the position of the ball. The school was founded in 1838 and was based at Benwell Dene when this photograph was taken.

Children doing Swedish drill at the Ponteland Cottage Homes, *c.* 1925. Note the maypole in the background. The homes housed orphans and children in need of care. They were built in 1901/02 by the Newcastle Poor Law Union.

Classrooms at Pendower Open Air School, 1925. Newcastle was one of the most overcrowded and unhealthy cities in the country during the interwar years. Healthcare was as important as education for children living in slum conditions. The school taught pupils with TB, rickets, anaemia and some physical handicaps. The best remedy was a regime of fresh air, sunshine, good food, exercise, rest and warm clothing.

Rutherford High School for Girls, 1949. This picture shows the fine Victorian buildings of the old school on Maple Terrace, now the site of Newcastle College. Both the grammar schools on this page sprang from the pioneering educational work of the Scottish preacher and social reformer, John Hunter Rutherford.

Rutherford Grammar School for Boys, 1957. J. Gibson breaks the tape at the first sports day held at the new school premises on the West Road. The school had been waiting to move from the historic but inadequate Bath Lane premises since the 1920s. Rutherford Grammar School was founded in 1877 as the School of Science and Art.

A carefully posed gymnastic display by Rutherford girls, 1953.

Six

Transport

A horse-drawn bus standing outside the Gateshead Industrial Co-operative Society branch in Wellington Street, Gateshead, c. 1920. This was the only public transport link across the river to Newcastle until 1923. The bus belonged to Works Contractors Ltd, 45 High Street West, Gateshead. The service lasted until 1933 and was known as the 'Ha'penny Lop'.

A horse-drawn furniture van belonging to John R. Graham of Gosforth, *c.* 1900. This was an advertising shot for the builders J. Davison, Albion Rolley Works, Byker.

A horse-drawn cab stands at the corner of Mosley Street and Pilgrim Street, 1902. The cab was incidental; the photograph was taken to show an extension to Newcastle Corporation Tramways' new electric track. The first rail was laid on 19 April 1900 and the system was fully operational by 1904. Power was supplied by a generating station at Manors.

A Class H tramcar, no. 21, outside the tram sheds. This class of tram was built between 1906 and 1910, to replace single-decker cars.

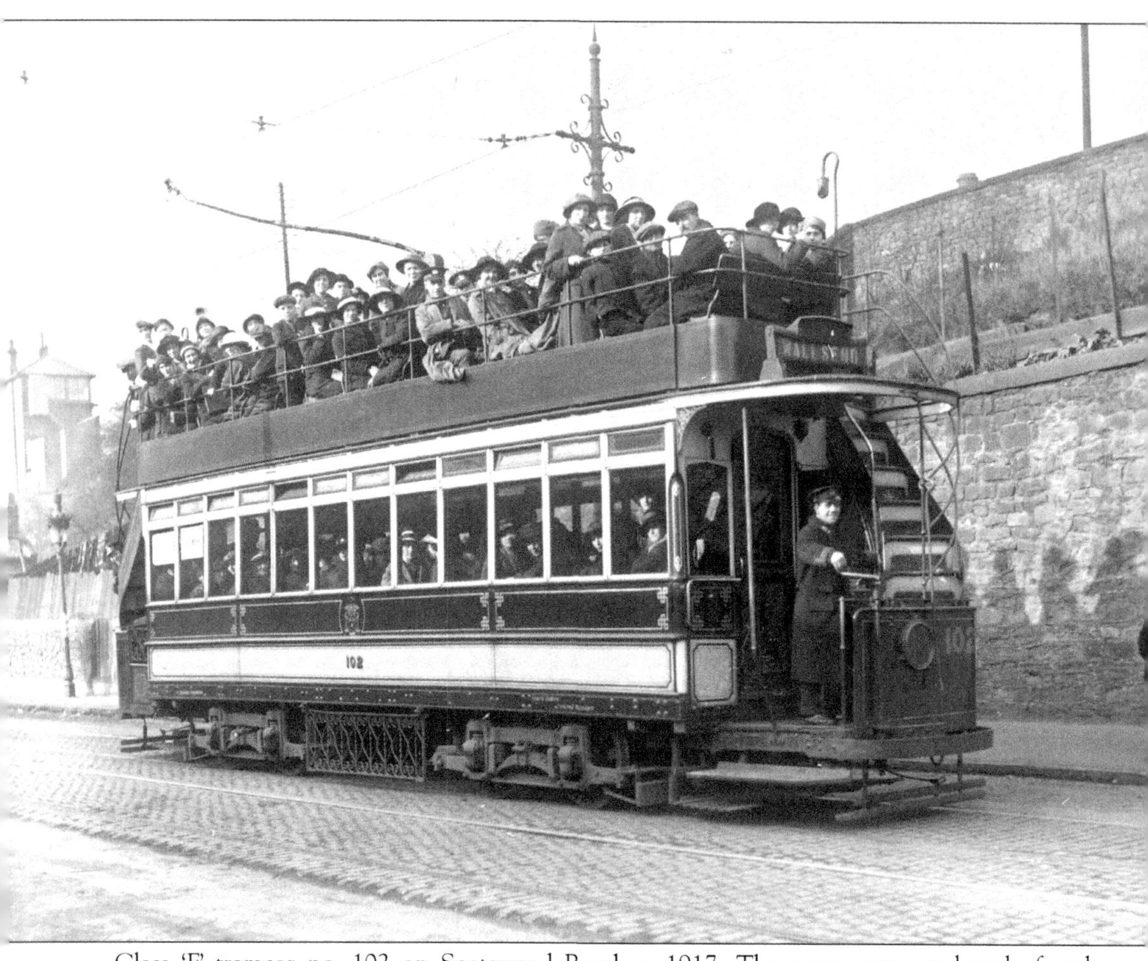

Class 'F' tramcar no. 102 on Scotswood Road, *c.* 1917. The passengers are largely female munitions workers from Armstrong's Elswick works.

The portico of Central station with St Mary's Cathedral, *c.* 1890. Designed by John Dobson, the station cost £90,000 and was opened by Queen Victoria on 29 August 1850. To cut costs the portico was not added until 1863.

Central station and Neville Street, *c.* 1920. Tramcars and motor vehicles have almost supplanted horse power by this stage.

Central station, *c.* 1860. The station was described by the architectural historian, Nikolaus Pevsner, as 'one of the best in England and better than any in London, save the much smaller Kings Cross.'

Platforms 7 and 8 of Central station, *c.* 1890. The elegant roof of the train shed is clearly shown. The original ribbed roof has three spans constructed from timber and glass, supported by slender cast-iron columns 7m high. Each rib is tied across its ends with a wrought-iron rod and linked by a wrought-iron hanger to the crown of the arch.

Railway crossings and the castle, *c.* 1920. When completed in the 1890s this busy junction at the east end of Central station was said to be the largest railway crossing in the world. The lines on the left carried the main-line services and the electric coast services (note the electric train on the extreme left), while those on the right crossed the High Level Bridge. This view also shows a spectacular piece of Victorian vandalism: the railway was cut through the castle bailey, only feet from the keep.

The first electric train between Benton and Newcastle, 27 September 1903. The North Tyneside Loop to Tynemouth and Whitley Bay opened the following year.

A Sentinel steam bus with trailer, 1919. It ran to Burradon during the week and was used at weekends to remove manure from the Corporation stalls, being cleaned in time for service on Monday mornings.

Travers' motor showroom, New Market Street, *c.* 1925. This was an early example of a specially designed 'motor sale-room for all types of cars'.

Freeing the Redheugh Bridge from tolls, 10 May 1937. The Lord Mayor and the Mayor of Gateshead met at the centre of the bridge, shook hands and declared it open for all time to come. The High Level Bridge was freed on the same day. The total cost of buying out the rights of the bridge companies was £275,000; half the sum was met by the Ministry of Transport.

A line-up of five Guy BTX trolleybuses at Stephenson's Monument, on the occasion of the opening of the trolleybus route to Denton Burn on 1 October 1935. When the Corporation decided to invest in trolleybuses, a powerful argument was that they would run on home produced fuel, 'generated at our own power station'.

A Corporation Daimler double-decker bus, *c.* 1935.

An abnormal load from Armstrong's negotiates the Swing Bridge, *c.* 1955. The Scammel low-loader is carrying a large knock out flare drum used in the chemical and oil industries.

The congested Tyne Bridge approach, 15 April 1964. The Victorian railway bridge was demolished and replaced by a wider concrete bridge as part of the Pilgrim Street roundabout scheme.

Pilgrim Street roundabout on 29 August 1967. Swan House is under construction.

Seven
Shops and Industries

The new Grainger Market, *c.* 1905. It was opened in 1835 to replace the existing market that was cleared during the building of Grey Street. Many of the original shop fronts still survive today.

Cassels clothing and hat shop at 45 Shields Road, 1870. Note the fine shop sign.

At its height, Shields Road offered an attractive alternative shopping centre to the main town. Beavan's store was a key part of this. This photograph shows the furnishing department block opposite the main shop. The front part of the building could only be two storeys high because it was built above the tunnel for the Riverside Branch of the London & North-Eastern Railway.

Beavan's store employees, *c.* 1910.
Note the number of young workers.

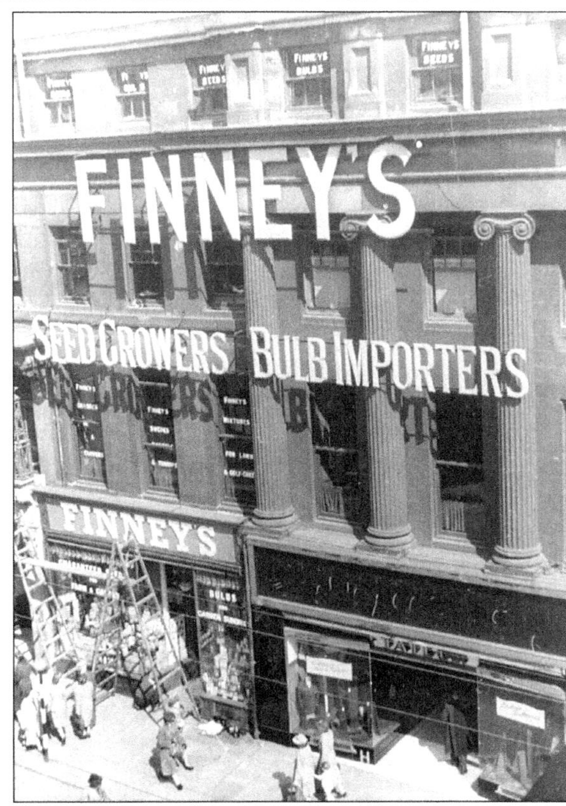

The shop and headquarters of Finney's
Seeds at 20 Grainger Street, 1937.
The company boasted that it was
the oldest seed firm in the country,
established in 1749. The trial grounds
for crops were at Stocksfield.

The interior of Bradley and Martin's, 1903. The well-known firm of wholesale and manufacturing chemists was based at 29 Mosley Street. This photograph was taken by Fred Penfold, an apprentice.

The Scientific Instrument Department at Bradley and Martin's in 1903. It looks rather like the laboratory of an Edwardian mad scientist!

Messrs Coxon's department store, Grey Street and Market Street, *c*. 1925. The century-old building had just been modernized with two new floors added to the Market Street elevation. The architects boasted that 'the floors are now spacious, abundantly lit, and there is a grace and charm about it all that pleases the customer, the shopkeeper and his assistants. This important store now has some semblance of modernity....'

Doric House, *c*. 1925. This shop was built for Robert Sinclair Ltd in 'the severely plain but refined style of the ancient Greeks, to complement its historic site near the castle'. It was an experimental building with a steel frame covered in terrazzo, marble chips set in fine cement and highly polished. The Greek medallions on the shop sign were a visual link to the firm's 'Tonides' brand of cigarettes.

The Crow's Nest Hotel, Barras Bridge, *c.* 1930.

The new White Horse sign is proudly displayed on the White Horse pub, Groat Market, 1951.

Hand-shaving skins at Richardson's leather works, 1898. Note the boy worker hidden at the back of the shot. The Company made a wide variety of products, including leather for bookbinding, handbags, shoes, gloves and belts for driving machinery.

One of the dirtiest jobs at Richardson's was reserved for women. This photograph of the glue pans was taken in around 1876. Waste hides, hooves and horn were boiled to make glue and nothing was wasted. Left-over hair was washed, dried and sold to builders to put into plaster.

Visit of HRH the Prince of Wales (later King Edward VIII) to Parsons' Heaton works in 1923. The Prince is being shown the assembly of a 500-watt turbine by Sir Charles Parsons. Parsons patented his revolutionary design for a steam turbine in 1884 and set up his own company at Heaton in 1889. These world-famous works came under foreign ownership in 1998.

Women workers prepare a group of 150cm searchlights, mounted on carriages, in 1943. During the Second World War Parsons' Heaton works adapted production to include gun cases, engine frames and machined parts for tanks and aircraft.

In 1928 Armstrong's merged with Vickers to become Vickers Armstrong Ltd. This photograph shows an export order for the same year: 2-6-0 locomotives built for the Egyptian State Railway being loaded onto a ship.

A wartime assembly line for Valentine tanks at the Elswick works. Now Challenger 2 tanks are made in Vickers' modern factory at Scotswood.

Two-decker pit cages in production at Vickers Armstrong, 1953. The plant at Elswick covered 70 acres and extended a mile along the banks of the Tyne. The company enjoyed boom years during the 1950s, manufacturing not only armaments but a vast range of engineering products including hydraulic presses, litho printing machines and industrial tractors. The National Coal Board, with almost 200 collieries in the Northern Division, was an active customer.

Vickers also manufactured items for shipbuilders. This crankshaft for a Doxford engine was heading for a Sunderland-built ship.

Eight

Sport and Leisure

The Amateur Rowing Club of the Elswick works and their supporters, *c.* 1900. The Tyne had a notable tradition of rowing competitions and produced great Victorian champions such as Harry Clasper.

The Newcastle Stock Exchange walk, 1903.

Young spectators keep pace with the competitors. No. 73 is showing the strain.

Newcastle Picture House, 10-12 Grey Street, on the eve of opening in 1914. By this time there were thirty cinemas in the city. The Picture House tried to convey the atmosphere of an exclusive club. A publicity brochure noted: 'There is an electric passenger lift for balcony patrons.... Leading from the first floor foyer is a handsome smoke room and café in the late seventeenth-century style.... For the convenience of patrons who are shopping, parcels may be addressed to the theatre to await their arrival or departure.'

Newcastle Empire auditorium, 1926. The cinema, with accommodation for 750 people, opened in 1913. It was converted from Dunn and Dick's jewellers shop by Moss Empires Ltd, who also owned the adjoining Empire Theatre. The site is now the Grainger Street entrance to the Newgate Shopping Centre.

The West End Bowling Club, 1890. What a fine collection of hats! The roof of Rutherford High School is on the right and St Mary's church is on the left.

Heaton Park Lawns, *c.* 1900. The park was given to the city by Lord Armstrong in 1879.

Newcastle Curling Club, *c.* 1890.

The famous stepping stones at the north end of Jesmond Dene, *c.* 1900.

Leazes Park and the New Royal Infirmary, *c.* 1905. This splendid city centre park was laid out in 1872 to cater for the city's booming population.

Two children feed the swans in Leazes Park in 1954.

The YMCA building on Blackett Street was opened by the Duke of Connaught on 10 May 1900. Facilities included a games room, a reading room, a hall with a capacity for 1,000 people and a gymnasium mounted on rubber buffers to muffle the noise.

The Sheriff, John Grantham, opens Benwell Billiard Saloon with a clean break, 28 November 1924.

A bevy of female cyclists from the Newcastle Road Club surround the Mayor at the beginning of the 'President's Run' to Shotley Bridge in 1936.

Councillor Mrs J. Grantham greets the English women's football team on 12 June 1938, after their recent victory over Scotland.

The two photographs on this page are enlargements of cigarette cards issued by the Ardath Tobacco Company, makers of State Express and Ardath cigarettes. Fenwick United, whose members were recruited from the shop workers, were formed in 1926 and were members of the Newcastle and District Traders' League.

Newcastle United, c. 1936. Alderman J. Lunn was chairman (front row, fifth from left) and S. Weaver was the captain (front row, fourth from right).

The FA Cup travelling up Grey Street in 1955, Newcastle FC's golden year. Local photographer Jimmy Forsyth took these atmospheric shots.

The Cup is carried in triumph round St James's Park.

Basketball in the Lightfoot Sports Centre, 1965. The centre was officially opened by Denis Howell on Wednesday 10 November of the same year. Those unused to the design might suspect a flying saucer had landed in Walker!

Judo practice and table tennis, 1965. The Lightfoot Centre brought a new sophistication to indoor sports facilities, with a large multi-use space.

The Hoppings began as the Newcastle upon Tyne Town Moor Temperance Festival in 1882, as a counter-attraction to the Summer Race meeting at Gosforth Park. The first festival lasted only two days but in subsequent years the fairground grew to fill a huge site on the town moor and earned the nickname 'the greatest show on earth'. This photograph shows the festival on Green Pool Field, Jesmond Vale, in 1923. The Jesmond site was used as a stop-gap from 1914 to 1923 because of a legal dispute between the Freemen and the Showmen over damage done to the moor by rolling stock during bad weather.

Civic dignitaries welcome the festival back to the Town Moor, 24 June 1923. By the 1930s it was estimated that, if the weather was good, 150,000 people visited the Hoppings each day.

The great wind-storm of 22 June 1927 struck just after the shows and stalls had been erected. From a fairground the Hoppings was turned into a nightmare of shattered wood and twisted metal.

The Haunted Castle, *c.* 1935. Ghost shows have long been a firm favourite.

Tiny Tim's coach in front of his show at the Hoppings, *c.* 1935. Harold Pyatt, better known as Tiny Tim, was born in 1887. As an adult he was 23 inches high and weighed 24lbs. He was 12 inches smaller than the more famous Tom Thumb.

Mary Ann Bevan's show on the Town Moor, *c.* 1935. She was born in London and worked as a farm labourer in Kent. She married and had four children in the years before 1914. After the death of her husband in the First World War, Ann dressed as a man to return to work on the land. When her sex was discovered she was sacked. Later she travelled different fairs as 'The World's Ugliest Woman'.

A Mickey Mouse theme for a roundabout, 1944. During the war the festival played an important part in the 'Holidays at Home' campaign.

The next four pictures show scenes from the Town Moor Festival in 1950/51. The 'Armless Wonder' was an old-fashioned freak show. The star, the son of a Welsh miner, demonstrated a series of accomplishments including using a typewriter, playing the xylophone and painting.

Cowboy movies were in vogue and some shows adopted the theme.

1951 saw the first visit of the hi-tech Rotor to the Town Moor.

These traditional gondola rides, once with names like 'Lusitania' and 'Mauretania', were re-christened to catch the flying saucer craze.

Nine

Social Problems and Social Care

The last patients being transferred by horse ambulance from the old infirmary on Forth Banks to the new Royal Victoria Infirmary at Castle Leazes.

The pictures on these two pages show the remarkable work of the Newcastle Wesleyan Methodist Mission in 1909. The dedicated church workers took a realistic view of the problems of faith in the inner city. With employment running at 14 per cent they admitted 'it is easier for a man to get beer than it is for him to get work, money and bread'. The Ouseburn district was typical when Pastor Reed reported, 'I have never known a more serious condition of things around City Road. Some who did come with us to worship are ashamed to appear in the mean clothing to which they have been reduced.' One attempt to 'slay the demon of want' was the Labour Yard.

During 1909, 400 men were given 6,000 days' work cutting 500 tons of wood into logs and bundles of firesticks. The Mission proudly announced that the project gave 'work, not mere charity'.

Children were the focus of special attention, but it was not always easy for church workers. They were warned. 'You must not object to children ill-clad and almost nil-clad.... Should you wish to scratch, you may do it unblushingly.'

Activities included Sunday school, Cripple's Guild and Children's Happy Hour, reaching out to 1,800 or 2,000 children a week. As the 1909 church report commented, 'you must be profoundly sorry, even to distress, at hundreds of little feet blue with the cold; then you must set your teeth and get on with the work.'

A visit to the pawn shop was a regular event for many Newcastle families at the turn of the twentieth century. This is a pawn shop on Scotswood Road in around 1910. Note however the barefoot boys in the entrance to the house above. The shop owners were not markedly better off then some of their customers.

In 1891 John H. Watson and John T. Lunn began the Newcastle Poor Children's Seaside Trips Association. On their first outing they took 120 impoverished children from their slum homes for a day at the seaside at nearby Monkseaton. By the 1930s their charity had been renamed the Poor Children's Holiday Association and Rescue Agency. The new title reflected a wide-ranging organization. Activities now included running a boys' rescue and training home, a night shelter for destitute boys, a street children's club and a farm colony at Stannington. These two shots show a Christmas party held at the Percy Street headquarters, *c.* 1934.

A PCHA day out to the seaside, 1936. A crocodile of excited children walk along Scotswood Road to Central station.

At the seaside, with the Tyne piers in the background. Bathing costumes were in short supply. The PCHA remains active today under the name of Children North East.

The children 'help' a local fishing boat on this seaside jaunt in the 1920s.

Newcastle's hospitals have long been regionally or even nationally famous. The state of the art Royal Victoria Infirmary continued this tradition. Here we see the laying of the foundation stone by HRH Albert Edward, Prince of Wales, on 20 June 1900. The New Infirmary was 'replete with all the requirements of a modern hospital providing accommodation for 400 in-patients, a home for 100 nurses, an Out-Patients' Department and rooms for clinical instruction.'

Number 2 Pavilion at the Royal Victoria Infirmary. There were eight pavilions altogether, each with surgical wards on the ground floor and medical wards on the first floor. Every ward had a kitchen, bathroom, day room, sister's room and a room for 'the examination of secretions'.

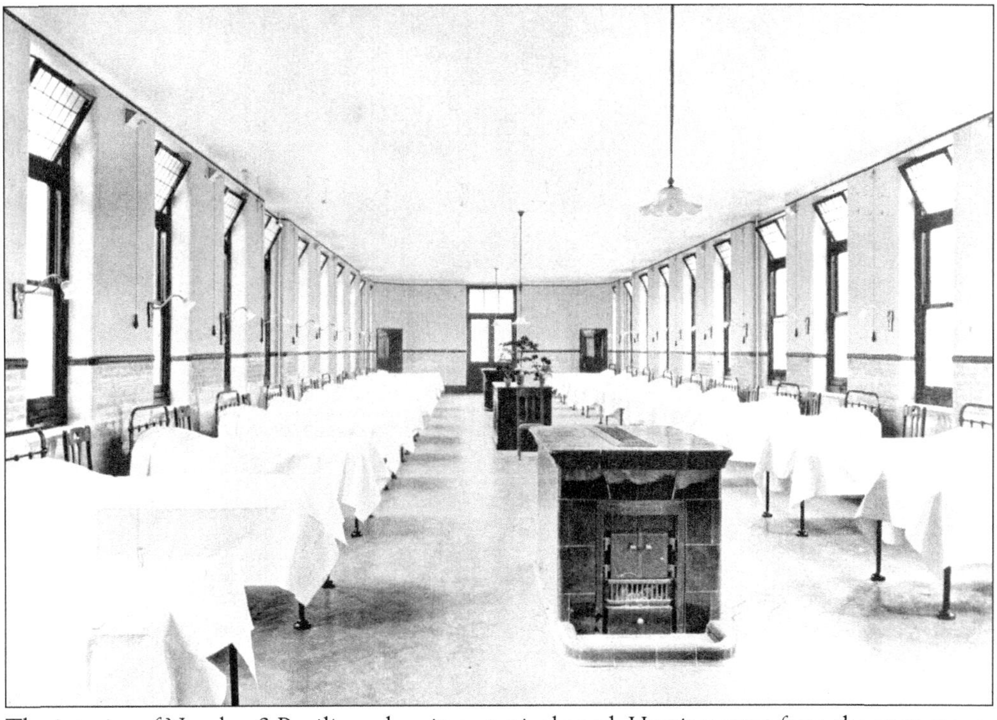

The interior of Number 2 Pavilion, showing a typical ward. Heating came from the open stoves and hot water radiators.

Switching hospitals to Newcastle General, the night staff get ready to perform amateur theatricals as 'The Hanky Panky Kids' in January 1918. Newcastle General was opened by the Poor Law Union as the Workhouse Hospital in 1870. During the war the workhouse and part of the hospital were taken over to treat servicemen suffering from venereal disease.

Newcastle General children's ward beautifully decorated for Christmas, *c*. 1910.

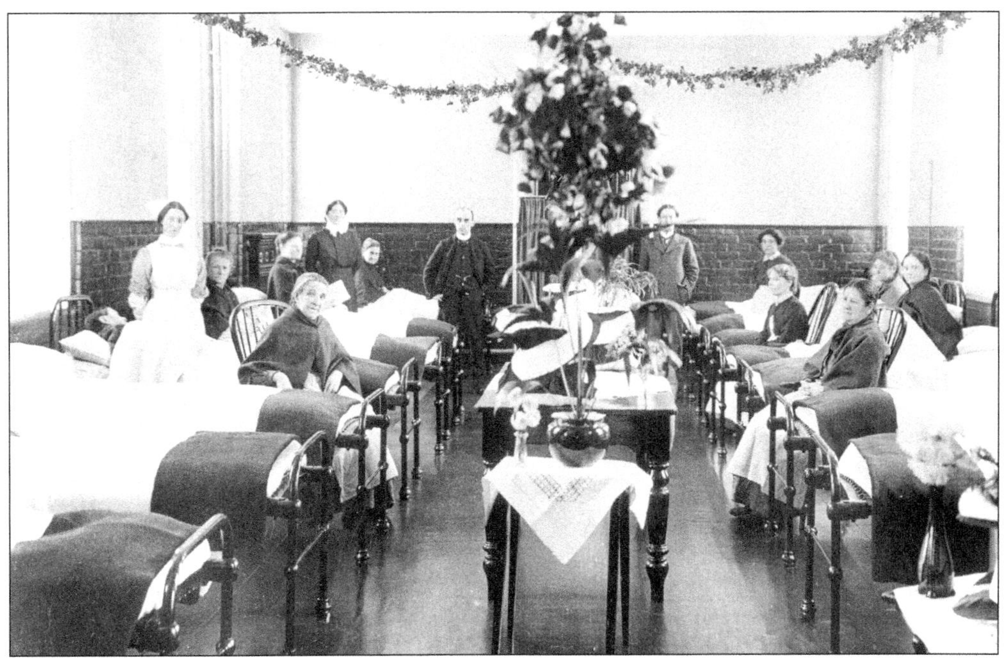

A female ward in Newcastle General, *c*. 1920. The formal pose and uniform dress of the patients indicate this was still a Poor Law institution.

Donated cots are the focus of this Christmas scene at the Fleming Memorial Hospital for sick children, 1946.

A fine array of toys welcomes the children on Christmas morning, 1946. The Fleming Memorial Hospital began life as the Children's Hospital, Hanover Square, in 1863. It was renamed after John Fleming, a Newcastle solicitor, donated £25,000 for a new building in memory of his wife. This opened at Moor Edge in 1882. After 100 years' sterling service the hospital closed in 1988 when its workload was transferred to the Fleming Wing of the Royal Victoria Infirmary.

Neville Chamberlain, Minister of Health, tours unhealthy areas of the city, 16 October 1925.

Crippled boys training as bootmakers at Sanderson Hospital, 1913. The hospital was founded as the Sanderson Home for Destitute and Crippled Children in 1888 and moved to Salters Road, Gosforth, in 1897.

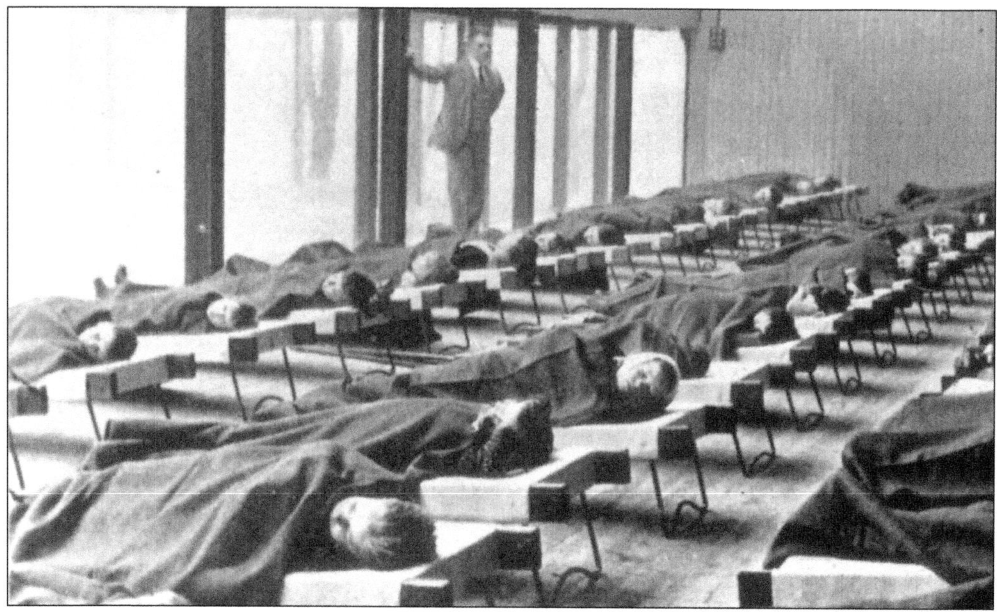

Children take a compulsory afternoon nap at Pendower Open Air School, 1925 (see also p. 58).

Poor children queuing with jugs in hand outside the Industrial Dwellings Soup Kitchen, Garths Head, in 1909. The kitchen was an emergency response to high unemployment in the All Saints area. In the week before Christmas, 800 loaves and 1,000 quarts of soup were distributed to deserving families.

Fifteen Basque refugee boys, victims of the Spanish Civil War, arrive in Newcastle, 28 June 1937.

Opposite: Children being treated with the new artificial sunlight equipment at the Northern Counties Chest Hospital, 1938.

NOTICE.

It should be clearly understood that this Hospital is a purely charitable institution, intended for the benefit of the poor only. The Medical Officers receive no payment for their services. All moneys received, whether from subscribers or from patients at the Hospital, are devoted solely to the cost of drugs and the maintenance of the Institution. Those who can afford to pay for medical treatment in the ordinary way are not eligible as Hospital patients.

The original notice board for the Northern Counties Hospital for diseases of the chest. This opened at 50 Blackett Street in 1878 as a private charity.

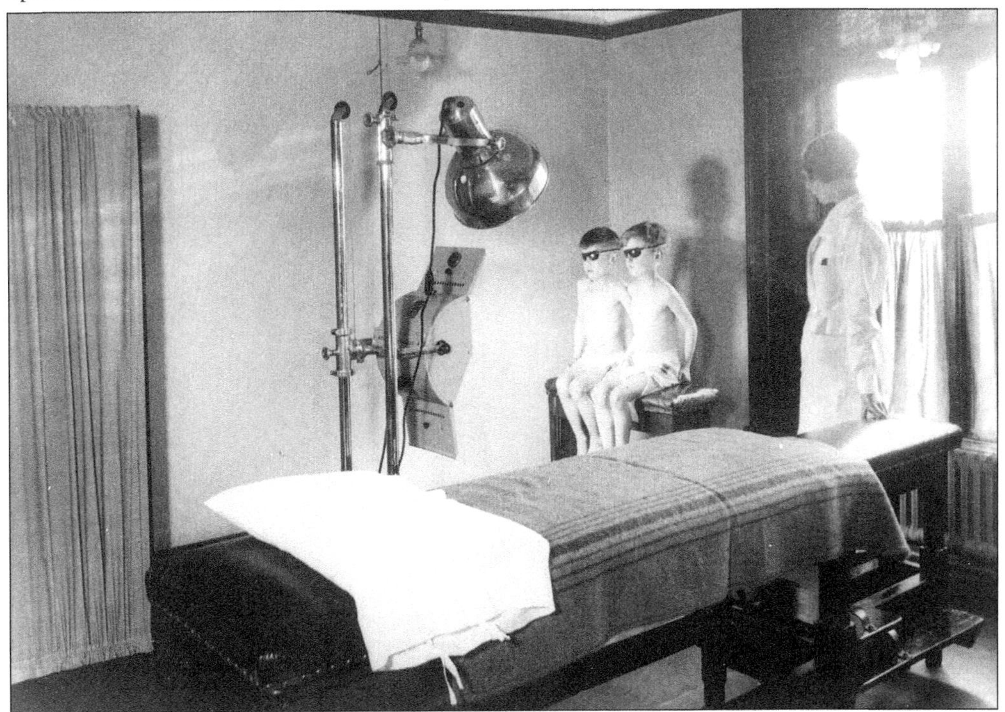

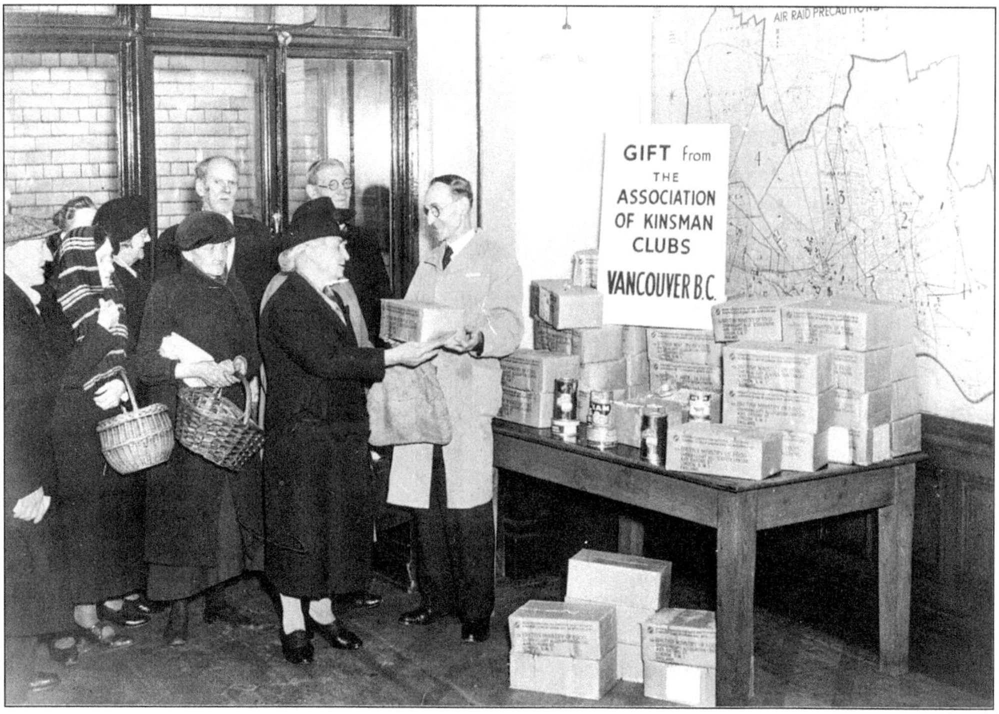

These two shots show the distribution of Canadian food parcels to old age pensioners on 10 August 1949. Rationing remained strict in the post-war years and gifts like these were a real treat. 29,000 parcels from the Dominions, the USA, Norway and Fiji were issued across the city.

Ten

Celebrations and Sorrows

The Mayor's barge alongside Mansion House Quay on Barge Day (Ascension Day), *c.* 1881. For hundreds of years civic processions on the river were a feature of city celebrations. In 1633, for example, King Charles I was treated to a river trip on the Mayor's barge. When Newcastle controlled the upkeep of the Tyne, the barge was used to conduct an annual survey from Spar Hawk at the river mouth to Hedwin Streams, seven miles west of Newcastle.

The last of the River Tyne state barges, launched from the yard of Messrs John Oliver at South Shields, on 6 May 1834. This craft was $51\frac{1}{2}$ft long by $10\frac{3}{4}$ft broad and needed a team of a dozen rowers. It was finally removed from the boathouse in the River Tyne Commissioners' Howdon Yard, and fixed on the lawn at Elswick House on 13 April 1903.

Newcastle Volunteer Horse Artillery parade through the city, 1903.

The Maxim Gun Section of the Northumberland Hussars on manoeuvres at Blagdon Park, the home of the Ridley family, June 1913. The Hussars were the local cavalry regiment. The Newcastle contingent trained at the Drill Hall on Northumberland Road, then an indoor riding school.

The outbreak of the First World War was welcomed on Tyneside. There was a splendid response to Lord Kitchener's appeal for more men. Here eager recruits are sworn in for the Tyneside Irish and Scottish battalions at the Corn Exchange, 12 November, 1914.

These four amateur snaps show scenes from the Victory March in Northumberland Street on Peace Day, 19 July 1919. This is the Royal Navy contingent. This was an Empire-wide celebration, with 10,000 troops on parade in Newcastle. They assembled on the Town Moor and began the march at eleven o'clock. An estimated crowd of 250,000 crammed the city to join in the celebrations. The Lord Mayor took the salute at the war memorial in Barras Bridge. At 10.40 that night a 42ft bonfire was lit on Cow Hill. In the dark another twenty-five huge bonfires could be seen burning in the distance.

Red Cross Nurses and members of the Voluntary Aid Detachment (known as VADs).

Wounded Tommies in wagons.

An aeroplane towed by an RAF truck.

The Royal Agricultural Show on the Town Moor, 1923. The Royal Victoria Infirmary is at the bottom left of the photograph.

The funeral of the victims of the Montague Colliery disaster. This shot shows the scene at the pit-head as the hearses leave in procession for Elswick Cemetery, 24 May 1925. The disaster happened when miners accidentally broke through to the flooded workings of a neighbouring abandoned colliery. Thirty-eight men died when the mine was inundated.

Part of the solemn procession along Elswick Road, 24 May 1925.

The North East Coast Exhibition held in 1929 was probably the greatest show ever to hit Newcastle. Its main purpose was to advertise northern industry and regenerate the local economy during a time of depression and intense foreign competition. It was a spectacular success with almost 4.5 million visitors. Attractions included the Palace of Engineering, the Himalayan Railway, the African Village and the Water Chute. These photographs were taken by the Sherlock family of Tynemouth during their visit. Here is the main entrance, at the crossroads of Park Terrace and Claremont Place: the designers cashed in on the fashion for all things Egyptian following the discovery of Tutankhamun's tomb.

A view of Main Avenue across the boating lake. The Palace of Industries is on the right and the Empire Marketing Board Pavilion on the left.

The bridge from the Palace of Arts to Main Avenue.

A closer view of Main Avenue. Simpson's confectioners have a stall on the left with the Empire Marketing Board Pavilion behind. This was designed as a showcase for the products of the Empire.

The Newcastle and Gateshead Gas Company offices, Grainger Street West, decorated for the Coronation of King George VI, 1937.

The Mayor's coach on Pilgrim Street during his tour of the city decorations celebrating the Coronation of King George VI, 8 May 1937.